JEALOUSY

A Psychologist's Guide to Overcome Envy, Codependency & Possessiveness in Any Relationship - Trust, Love & Be Happy

KATHERINE CHAMBERS

TABLE OF CONTENTS

INTRODUCTION

"You can be the moon and still be jealous of the stars"

(Gary Allan)

Human beings typically operate from two default positions. We are either striving to better ourselves or conserving what we have in a survival type mode. It doesn't take much to understand which of these is most beneficial for our mental state. The former involves a small degree of envy from time to time, whilst the latter promotes jealousy for the most part. One drives us forward, the other holds us back.

Regardless of how emotionally stable you currently are, we all have a tendency to act in ways which aren't in our best interests on occasions, which includes jealous behavior. It's inescapable. Fortunately it's usually only for brief spells when we are adolescents and less consciously aware of the consequences of our actions. Although we often grow out of this phase in time, but remember nobody is perfect.

I like to break these psychological principles down into the simplest of terms to really get to the bottom of them. To shine a light onto what we are dealing with here. In reality, counteracting jealous thinking patterns is about doing two things in general:

1. Identifying the underlying causes of your frustrations and triggers which promote this type of behavior

2. Learning the psychological strategies to defend against and downplay them when they do arise.

This is of course easier said than done. I have certainly had my fair share of bad relationships and bouts of jealousy along the way. Dealing with these instances becomes a journey like every other psychological self-development path you will find yourself on. But like any other, it will be well worth the time and effort you will put into fixing it.

Again, the key is in identifying the causes of your feelings, to fully recognize and take responsibility for them. To see them for what they are, an outward expression of some deeper cognitive dissonance in your mind. When you can do this, you can go about constructively reducing the negative impact they have on your life.

My aim for this book is to both layout the principles and concepts behind the feelings of envy and jealousy, but more importantly, to give you the knowledge and tools to better deal with them when they show up. To lessen the impact they have on your life in an adverse manner, and even ways to make them work in your favor to ensure your future relationships flourish.

Its not about being hard on yourself for feeling the way you do. This is somewhat out of your control. Its about working on the period which follows these feelings so they do not have such a debilitating effect on you. The following chapters will do just that, so approach this with a fresh and open mind and hopefully you will gain some insights to ultimately lead a more harmonious and jealous free life going forward.

MY CREDENTIALS

Before we get into deconstructing jealous behavior, it's probably a good idea to explain exactly who I am, and why you should even bother listening to me in the first place. Yes I have the undergraduate and master's degree in psychology from Stanford, but my main focus over the past 15 years has been on the practical elements of the discipline. I wouldn't call myself a "Self-Help Guru" but I do focus much more on the results of these principles in the real world, compared to my previous life of studying endless academic research papers on the subject.

I use what I have learned and observe the behavior and psychological patterns of other successful people in life, to pin point exactly what it is they are doing to elicit the results they are achieving. There are common patterns to these people and behaviors if you know how to spot them. Fortunately for you, even if you don't, I have spent the past 2 decades working this stuff out for you. I have dedicated my 40's to documenting both the rationale behind the most important psychological mindsets, as well as the practical advice on how to cultivate the ability to use them to your own benefit.

So why am I now writing a book on jealousy? As I mentioned, I studied a wide range of topics within the field of psychology and neuroscience at college, which formed my base understanding of these principles. But I have since picked up many critical skill sets whilst building a family and career of my own. Everything from managing my personal and business relationships to my own mental state. Everything has been a learning curve and one which has taken deep emotional understanding and soul searching at times.

I am not a marriage or relationship counsellor by any means. I just have much experience studying various psychological considerations which comprise our mental make-up. I have also had much life experience when it comes to building relationships, good and bad.

So now that you know a little more about me, let's dive in. The following chapters will give you a sound overview of the jealousy principles, as well as advice on how to overcome them. Similar to anger management and manipulation exercises, much of this work involves identifying the underlying issues you have, and the triggers which set off negative thinking in the first place. So make sure you are as open and honest with yourself when going through these techniques. I promise you, it will be well worth it.

PART 1: A BASIC UNDERSTANDING OF JEALOUSY & ITS PRINCIPLES

CHAPTER 1: DEFINING JEALOUSY – WHAT IS IT REALLY?

"Jealousy. A sentiment which is born in love and which is
produced by fear that the loved person
prefers someone else"

(Emile Littre)

In its base sense, jealousy is an emotion which refers to feelings and thoughts of insecurity, concern, resentment, anger, or fear over something of personal value. It is often associated with and used interchangeably with envy. However, whilst being somewhat synonymous with one another, these two terms do have slightly different meanings. These nuanced differences will be explored later within this chapter.

Jealousy is commonly experienced in a myriad of situations, such as the workplace, between siblings and within friendships just to name a few. For the purpose of this book however, we will focus on the type of jealousy which is evident in romantic and intimate relationships. As this is the most predominant place you will encounter it. Lets be honest, this is where it's debilitating hooks dig into us and do the most harm.

No one is completely immune to the green eyed monster, it seems innate and natural within us all. In fact, it has been observed in babies as young as five months old! Researchers claim that jealousy is evident in all societies and cultures, regardless of environmental factors such as upbringing. In truth, jealousy is a complex emotion. It strikes both women and men alike, although is commonly thought to be a female trait. Again, it is usually aroused whenever an individual perceives a threat, real or not, to a valued personal or professional relationship from a third party.

Can Jealousy Actually be a Good Thing?

According to evolutionary psychologists, jealousy should not be suppressed entirely. It has to be considered as a wake-up call or signal. Anyone who experiences these feelings should be on high alert that a relationship maybe in danger and that the necessary steps should be taken to assess the situation. In this sense, jealousy is a vital emotion since it maintains social bonds. In addition, it motivates individuals to engage in behaviors that preserve important relationships. Its the canary in the coal mine so to speak, which can signal that something might be amiss between you and your partner.

Dr. Helen Fisher, an anthropologist and author of the book *Why We Love*, states that a little jealousy can be healthy in relationships. It can serve as a reminder that your partner is attractive and that you are fortunate to have them. I'm not saying you should become submissive in anyway, but a little gratitude for what you have can go a long way. But as per usual, its the extremes in emotions which begin to hurt us most. Its when jealousy becomes chronic, overt and debilitating.

Dr. Lauren Papp, a professor in human development and family studies at the University of Wisconsin, suggested that chronic jealousy is a huge red flag and that people should stop mistaking it for interest, care, or affection. Many people seem to believe that their partners are more interested or in love with them if they are possessive or jealous. The reality, however, is that jealousy is almost always a sign of insecurity.

Jealousy vs Envy

With regards to jealousy, a third party is typically involved. This person is viewed as a rival for the affection one seeks. On the other hand, envy only occurs between two individuals. It occurs when a person wishes to have what the other one has, in a keeping up with the Joneses type mentality.

Hence, you experience envy whenever you see someone else obtaining what you desire. You harbor a feeling of resentment as you grave that particular object or position. You covet your neighbors new car or a friends promotion at work for example. However, such feelings do not necessarily equate to full blown jealousy. You may be envious of another persons situation, but still retain a good relationship with them.

For instance, your friend was able to lose weight after getting on a particular diet. So, you become envious of her achievement. However, instead of being jealous, you ask the person which diet plan she was on and perhaps attempt it for yourself. You become motivated to achieve a similar weight loss goal. Your envy caused you to become a progressive action taker, so in this sense, it can be a positive driver towards improvement.

Jealousy on the other hand, is predominantly negative and regressive. It can be dangerous, especially for those who are unable to control themselves. A highly jealous person typically directs their ill will towards a third party who is perceived to be receiving the affection or accolades they want for themselves. If he/she cannot have it, then the other person cannot have it either. Its negative energy which takes away more than it contributes in a zero-sum game mentality.

Chronic jealousy prevents us from moving forward. It consumes time and energy, as well as leads us down a destructive path if it's not curtailed quickly enough. It also involves a sense of entitlement. It makes you believe that you have the right to control the happiness of other people. Thus, it can lead to abuse. It is not caused by strong love, but rather by a sense of self-preservation.

What Causes A General Sense of Jealousy?

Many societies regard jealousy as a natural reaction to the sharing of something important or sacred with another person. However, this is a huge misconception. The real root of jealousy is not the sharing of special things. Its the feelings which these circumstances bring about. It's a sense that something has been lost or taken away from you. Jealous people do not want to share the things they perceive as valuable to them through fear of losing them. Its a protective mechanism which typically backfires on the person sooner rather than later.

In a romantic relationship, this "special thing" is typically the other party. For instance, a woman may become jealous when she sees her spouse giving another woman attention. Likewise, a man may become jealous when he hears his girlfriend profess positive things about another man. In these instances, the affected partner sees the other individual or the third party as a threat.

Below are some of the most common causes of jealousy:

1. Fear

Indeed, jealousy is heavily rooted in fear. However, there are various forms of fear we must address. In romantic relationships, the constant worry of losing a new partner is frequently experienced. For example, a woman who has been cheated on by an ex-husband may become highly cautious with her new partner as she fears that the same incident might happen again. She displays jealous behavior because she does not want to lose her new partner.

2. Insecurity or lack of self-confidence

If you do not believe you are worthy of being loved in return, you may believe that your partner will always want to be with someone else. This can occur due to low levels of self-esteem and self-confidence, which is almost always developed in childhood. You may have grown to be insecure due to unsupportive, unloving, or lack of caring parents when you were young. You may have also grown up in an environment wherein people often tried to mock or belittle you. Don't worry, we will explore the notion of raising overall self-esteem later in the second part of this book, as it is critical for overcoming jealous behavior.

3. Comparison

This concept also ties in very closely with a general sense of insecurity and lack of self-confidence. A person who constantly compares himself/herself with other people is likely to become jealous much easier. Likewise, a person who often feels that he/she is not good enough, can grow to resent the people whom they believe are better than they are.

The Common Signs of Jealousy Within a Romantic Relationship

When you experience jealousy, it has been shown that your emotions actually cause you to become somewhat mentally unstable. You may start to feel worthless. This can cause you to do unreasonable things. Thus, it is crucial to know the signs and symptoms and determine if you are experiencing them. This way, you can avoid acting in a way or saying things that you may regret later on down the line. You can inoculate yourself from the worst aspects of this type of behaviour by simply staying vigilant to the signs that you are heading down this path.

Keep in mind that you are a person worthy of love and affection. There is no need for you to be jealous of anybody. A romantic relationship cannot survive chronic jealousy. You have to know the difference between out-of-control envy and a healthy concern. The following are the most common signs that you are taking things too far:

1. Constant "checking up"

If your partner does not know where you are, he/she might call you as they are simply concerned for your safety and security. This kind of behavior is healthy and normal. However, when your partner checks on you constantly by texting or calling every hour of every day, they may be exhibiting unhealthy and jealous behavior. Your partner may be feeling insecure. Bear in mind that healthy couples in well functioning relationships do not feel the need to constantly check up on their partners. They feel secure in their relationships and retain trust at all times.

2. Looking through phones and other personal belongings

If you are in a healthy romantic relationship, then there is no need for you to look through the personal belongings of your partner, such as his/her phone or social media accounts. You trust the person, so you do not believe that he/she will cheat on you or leave you. If you are committed and happy, there is no fear of infidelity. On the other hand, if you are extremely insecure or jealous, you may look through your partner's stuff for evidence of cheating.

3. Constant accusations

If you are in a loving relationship, you will not feel the need to flirt with anyone else. You and your partner both feel this way. However, if you are in an unhealthy relationship, you may regularly accuse your partner of flirting or cheating. You do not feel secure and your jealousy drives you to have unreasonable thoughts and make irrational claims.

How to Deal with Jealousy

The latter part of this book will deal more thoroughly with the practical steps one must take to adequately deal with chronic jealously effectively. For now, lets just say that during these situations, you and your partner need to have a serious and frank conversation. You have to assure one another that loyalty and commitment must be front and center within the relationship. It is important to address any problems or misunderstandings from the outset.

In addition, you have to take note of any signs that may indicate an abusive relationship. If you notice these red flags, you must evaluate your situation very carefully and decide whether to solve the problem or perhaps move on. Sometimes, exiting the relationship is the best option. You have to get out of a potentially harmful situation before it gets out of hand. I explore how to identity these signs more deeply with *"Manipulation: A Psychologists Guide"*.

It is true that jealousy can sometimes be justified. For example, if you cheated on your spouse, then you can expect him/her to have a hard time trusting you again. Then again, even though infidelity has already played a role in your marriage, you should still refrain from being controlling. You should not display any jealous behavior as this will just make your relationship worse.

You and your partner can either choose to save your marriage and start over, or file for divorce. For many folks, ending the relationship is the easier option. They can find peace of mind as they no longer have to suffer trust issues with the same person. For others, having a mature conversation and saving the relationship remains the preferable option as they may have children and shared properties for instance. You should never stay with someone for these reasons alone, but they can be deciding factors in whether to give things a second chance.

Even though the trust is gone, you can bring it back again with a little work. To do this, you need to evaluate the behavior of your partner and determine if this person is truly trustworthy and worth a second shot. You have to examine his/her history, such as incidents of cheating. You have to determine if your partner is the kind of person to always find an excuse for their behavior or does not show remorse. If they do these kinds of things, then they may not be worth the effort.

See to it that you evaluate your decisions very carefully in this respect. You have to determine whether to push through or just quit the relationship. Your state of mind is very important, and if you cannot trust your partner, then you will always feel insecure and jealous.

Refrain from playing mind games as they do nothing but further reduce the trust in the relationship. It will simply ensure that your partnership will worsen over time. Bear in mind that relationships need two people to function properly. If you are constantly playing mind games, you undermine the very nature of what you are trying to achieve. The whole must be greater than the sum of the parts. So don't self-sabotage the bond you are creating by continually second guessing one another.

Refrain from letting your imagination run wild. For instance, if your spouse comes home late, don't immediately assume that he/she went out to see the "other" party. But rather give your partner the benefit of the doubt, afford them time to explain where they were. Do not assume the worst in every situation. Avoiding negative thinking spirals is imperative to a healthy and functioning relationships.

A wild imagination can be highly damaging to your partnership. So try to remain grounded and realistic. If your significant other has always been loyal to you, then you should listen to their explanations. A healthy relationship is built on trust remember, something I wont apologies for repeating many times in this book.

In addition to this, you should refrain from becoming too possessive. Always be aware that your partner is still his/her own person. Even though you have a common bond, you still do not own the other person. He/she has the right to live their own life on their own terms. Enough space is critical to maintain affection and attraction between one another. I often equate it to the earth and moon. Each body is connected in an everlasting orbital dance with one another, but with enough space to continually view the others wonder.

With that said, you should not prevent your partner from doing the things they love to do, such as pursuing their own hobbies and interests, as well as maintaining friends and associates outside of your shared social groups. Again, this aids in providing that slight but essential breathing space between the two of you, illustrating the fact that you are still indeed individual people. If you choose to share everything with each other at the end of the day, that is up to you.

However, it is not acceptable to become upset over trivial things. If you become jilted over these instances, you simply become fearful, insecure, and jealous for no reason. You may start to exhibit unreasonable and controlling behaviors. You need to be very self-aware in this respect and notice your own thinking patterns and actions. You also have to educate yourself on how to control your emotions. The following chapter will explain some of these traits in greater detail.

CHAPTER 2: TRAITS OF HIGHLY JEALOUS PEOPLE – HOW TO SPOT THEM IN YOURSELF & OTHERS

"Jealousy is troublesome to others, but a torment to themselves"

(William Penn)

According to Esther Boykin, a marriage and family therapist, every person experiences jealousy at some point in their lives, its unavoidable. However, it is important to identify these situations, to determine these feelings and not let them control our behaviors in an unhealthy manner.

The following are the most common traits of highly jealous people:

1. Highly jealous people want their partner all for themselves.

You may view this as passionate and romantic if your partner wishes to spend every waking a sleeping second with you and you alone. However, this kind of isolation is not healthy. At first, you may not view it as so. After all, everything seems loving, exciting, and passionate to begin with.

The truth is that the attempt to exert control and the underlying insecurity can never make a love affair last. It is not in a persons best interest to continually insist that their partners spend all their time with them. Unhealthy jealousy can quickly race out of hand and turn into an controlling and stifling situation in no time.

2. Highly jealous people are very emotionally dependent and "needy"

Salama Marine, a well renowned psychologist, states that high levels of emotional dependency are among the most telling signs of extreme jealousy. Highly jealous people do not want to be alone, even if they are no longer happy in their relationship. They are afraid to face the unknown.

Due to this fear, those people behave in extremely jealous ways. They also constantly ask and seek for reassurance. They believe their value relies on the presence of their partner. In short, they have very low levels of self-esteem.

3. Highly jealous people disapprove of their partner's hobbies, pastimes, and/ or dreams.

According to Michele Paiva, a neuromarketing strategist and Zen psychotherapist, other people are not the only threats which highly jealous people perceive. They are also threatened by things, places, hobbies, and goals. Yes this may in fact fall more accurately under the banner of envy. But I am including them here as they fall into the scope of a romantic relationship. As in these folks are threatened by anything that might take their partner away from them.

So, if their significant other enjoys musical plays for instance, they may elicit mocking behavior in an attempt to dissuade them from continuing to pursue them. If their partner begins engaging in a new hobby, they feel threatened as they believe their partner is capable of finding happiness without them. In this respect, they prevent the other person from growing and achieving their full potential.

4. Highly jealous people require total control over their partner.

In essence, they attempt to control the lives of their partner. According to Dr. Jennifer Rhodes, a dating expert and psychologist, the extreme jealousy of these individuals drives them to act in a controlling and scary manner. They tend to accuse their partners of flirting or cheating, demand to know their whereabouts, and again, check their phone.

They also become visibly stressed on seeing their partners talk to strangers. For instance, they may clench their fists or teeth. They may also prevent their partners from making new friends or even connecting with old ones. They restrict their freedoms in an unacceptable and ultimately damaging way.

5. Highly jealous people want their partner to behave a certain way.

Along similar lines to the above, these people expect their partner to do everything in line with their tastes, including the manner in which they behave and speak. They feel justified when they are able to control the actions of their partner in this way. However, this illustrates a large lack of respect and often leads to damaging back-lashing behavior in return.

In addition, they demand that their partners always stay in touch. If a phone call is not answered immediately for instance, they become angry and agitated as a result.

6. Highly jealous people give up their own lives just to stick to their partner.

It's not simply a case that highly jealous folks put stipulations on the lives of their partners. These people often do similar things to themselves. They stop doing the things they love, such as fulfilling their own life desires and purposes as they are anxious that this may negatively effect the relationship. They often abandon their own professional goals just to align more closely with their partner. This is a huge mistake.

Remember that you cannot love other people if you do not love yourself. And you cannot love yourself if you do not allow yourself to be happy by living your own life and engaging in activities that bring you fulfillment and joy. If you want some clearer guidance on exactly how to navigate these concepts better, then the following chapter on codependency will teach you just that.

CHAPTER 3: CODEPENDENCY, ATTACHMENT & COMMITMENT – BECOMING ADDICTED TO OTHER HUMANS

Its a widely known fact that the human brain is not fully developed for at least 18 years. Financial and psychological independence from parents takes at least this long. In addition to this, adults become dependent on one another for emotional and social needs, such as communication, friendship, love, appreciation, and nurturing. The closer people get, the more interconnected they become. They require greater levels of safety, security, comfort and proximity which can often lead to codependency.

There is this huge misconception that because humans are wired for dependency, it is normal for them to be codependent. Such a thing, however, is not healthy for relationships as we've already seen. Codependents are essentially relationship addicts. They are merely addicted to their partners as opposed to actually being in love. They relate to other people in an unhealthy manner, with patterns of self-sacrifice, obsession, control, and dysfunctional communication. They often abuse their partners or let themselves be abused as a consequence.

Couples who are codependent are not balanced. They often struggle for control and power, whilst commonly becoming resentful and anxious. They may even feel responsible for the moods and feelings of their partner. They attempt to control their partner to have their needs met. Instead of respecting the individuality of the other person, they cannot tolerate disagreement. They blame each other for causing problems, and do not take any form of personal responsibility.

In spite of the pain they experience, they remain in the relationship due to the fear of not being able to function alone. They have a mutual insecurity and codependency that makes outside intimacy threatening to them. Just like trees, they may seem mentally, emotionally, and physically independent on the surface. However, at an unconscious level, they are insecure and dependent on each other down to the roots.

This is why many of these people end up marrying those whose personality is different from their own. For example, a man who has difficulty expressing anger may marry a woman who has no difficulty expressing it herself Conversely, a woman who is closed off may marry a man who is gregarious by nature. A man who is financially wealthy may also marry a woman who is broke as he needs to take care of someone in order to feel worthwhile and needed. His partner, on the other hand, feels valued and loved in return.

Understanding Codependency

The term "codependency" can be defined as seeking love to repair one's feelings of inadequacy. As previously mentioned, people who are in codependent relationships are not in a good spot, as they have to fulfill the roles their partners expect them to fulfill. This form of security and unconditional love is actually a benefit and desirable for any healthy and normally functioning relationship to flourish. Its when this becomes an unwavering dependency which is the problem.

This is due to codependents typically having lower levels of self-esteem and high levels of insecurity. Hence, they find it difficult to stay true to themselves. They do everything to please their partner. They want to make sure they will be loved, so they sacrifice their own needs to meet the needs of their significant other.

A relationship which involves physical, psychological, and verbal abuse is characterized by sadomasochistic tendencies. The couple may remain in the relationship due to their fear of abandonment. For them, being alone is far worse than being abused.

So how can you identify if you have a loving relationship or a codependent one? The answer to this question is fairly simple. If you are always submerging your own wants for the wants of your partner due to your fear of asserting what you actually want. If you find yourself in this kind of situation, then you are in a highly self-destructive situation.

Both men and women are susceptible to these kind of relationships. However, women are more vulnerable to becoming victims. For instance, a woman may always meet men who do not wish for commitment. These men may even tell her right from the start that they do not want to get married or become an item. However, the woman remains in the relationship out of hope he will have a change of mind over time, which may or may not be the case.

As a result, the woman becomes highly sensitive to rejection. In fact, she expects to be rejected due to her previous experiences with similar men. She becomes paranoid and constantly seeks reassurance. In the beginning, she may be given this, however, over time, her partner goes on business trips and vacations that make her feel insecure and abandoned. This may cause her to implement even greater demands on her partner, degrading the overall relationship whilst increasing the codependency.

Since the man she's with is not generally interested in having an exclusive relationship, he may start to pull away due to her nagging and unpleasant behavior. If he does this, she may feel inclined to be even more demanding. If this continues, their relationship can have a disastrous ending. Even if the man actually ends up marrying the woman out of familiarity, the feelings of insecurity will only harbor and foster as time goes by.

This is just one example of a codependent relationship. There are many variations. However, the main tenet across all forms involves a sense of needing to be loved and taken care of. In extreme cases a person will tell the other that they will die if they are not taken care of. This can gilt trip the more stable individual into doing everything to avoid this. Both then become intertwined in an unhealthy standoff of simply staving off this worst case scenario.

Individuals who end up becoming codependents typically grow up in dysfunctional homes where their needs for affection and love were not met. So, they attempt to satisfy such needs vicariously by showering their significant others with love and attention. They give the love and attention that they never received but still really grave in return.

They also tend to choose partners who are needy, emotionally unavailable, angry, depressed or grieving. They may also choose partners who somewhat reflect their childhood experiences. For instance, if they had a parent who was angry, abusive, or emotionally unavailable when they were young, they will find a partner who exhibits similar characteristics.

In addition, they often try to "save" or "heal" their partners by giving them all of their wants and needs. Love addicts and codependents typically mold themselves into whatever their partners may want them to become. Their worst fear is being abandoned. So, they do everything in their power to avoid this, even if this means sacrificing their own needs and self-respect.

They even take care of the duties of their partner, such as doing their chores, taking care of their health needs, finding them a job, or even working for them. They basically become slaves to their partner. They also put up with the abusive tendencies as they believe that such behavior is in line with their self-worth. They may even put their partner before their own children. This is how addicted its possible to become and how dependent a relationship can get.

Codependents become highly focused on the fantasy of their relationship instead of the reality. They tend to ignore the dysfunctional or abusive traits of their partner as they choose to see only the potentials. They keep making excuses for their significant other in order to conceal the reality of the relationship. They do not mind lying, downplaying and covering up for their partner in front of family and friends.

In addition, these codependents feel satisfied when they do everything for their partner. Since their own childhood was full of chaos and control, they grew up with a sense of false security. They put all of the focus and attention on their partner and away from their own turmoil and inner pain. They do not work on themselves as it seems easier to work on their partner and the relationship instead. This is a mistake. Everything ultimately starts with you. Self-love becomes before everything.

Understanding Attachment

In reality, there are four types of attachment: secure, dismissive-avoidant, fearful-avoidant, and anxious-preoccupied. Your attachment style can affect your relationship as well as the intensity of your attachment style, which can change over time. Here are the rough breakdowns of each category:

Secure

People with a secure attachment style are emotionally intelligent. They are able to convey their emotions constructively and appropriately. They are able to send and receive expressions of intimacy in a healthy manner. Likewise, they are able to draw reasonable and appropriate boundaries. They feel secure, whether they are single or in a relationship.

In addition to this, these individuals have an optimistic view of personal interactions intimate or otherwise. When a problem occurs, they choose to discuss it rather than attack their partner. They are able to deal with interpersonal difficulties with ease. They also stay resilient during relational dissolution's. They grieve, learn, and move on. This is essentially where you want to get to.

Anxious-Preoccupied

People with this kind of attachment style are typically insecure and nervous about romantic relationships. They stress over many things, most of which merely comes from their imagination. This stress manifests itself through various problems, such as possessiveness, mood swings, obsessiveness, hypersensitivity, neediness, and jealousy.

These people do not easily give others the benefit of the doubt. They immediately harbor negative thoughts regarding the intentions of others. They will only feel accepted and secure after being continuously shown validation and love. They do not respond positively to regular and constructive feedback. They tend to have histories of problematic relationships and don't want to be alone.

They may even become dramatic and purposely cause relationship troubles simply to seek acceptance, attention, validation, and reassurance. Most of these folks actually feel more comfortable in a chaotic relationship. A peaceful and calm union feels unnatural for them.

Dismissive-Avoidant

People with a dismissive-avoidant attachment style are usually very self-sufficient and self-directed. They avoid genuine intimacy, which is also why they have very few real friends. They prefer to be emotionally and physically independent. Because of this, they often feel restricted in relationships. They tend to push away their partners when they get too close.

These people tend to have commitment issues. They would rather be single and alone as opposed to being in a subpar marriage or with a less than perfect romantic partner. They put everything else first, such as their friends, hobbies, and career, over their romantic relationships. This may also lead to narcissistic or passive-aggressive behavior in more extreme cases.

Fearful-Avoidant

People with this type of attachment style often suffer from abandonment, abuse, and other difficulties in life. They want to experience intimacy, but they resist it. They have high levels of inner conflict. They also struggle with relying on other people.

Moreover, they fear emotional and physical annihilation in romantic relationships. They tend to be suspicious of the intentions, actions, and words of their partner, as well as push them away when they begin to get closer.

How Attachment Styles Affect Relationships

Your attachment style can affect everything in your relationship, from your choice of partner to the way your relationship starts and ends. This is why it is crucial for you to recognize your attachment style. You have to learn about your vulnerabilities and strengths in order to be your best self in a relationship. Your attachment pattern is formed during early childhood and continues to serve as a working model for your adult relationships.

Your attachment style affects the way you react to your needs as well as how you get them met. If you have a secure attachment style, you are confident and able to interact with other people more easily. You also choose a partner who is similar to you. This is typically the healthy way to do things. On the other hand, if you have an avoidant or anxious attachment style, you may choose a partner who will not make you happy in the long run.

For instance, if you have an anxious attachment style, you may choose a partner who is isolated or difficult to connect with. You choose this kind of person as you feel that you have to be with them at all times to foster this bond. On the other hand, if you have an avoidant attachment style, you may choose someone who overly demands for attention or is possessive. You go for this type of person as you feel you should behave as if your needs are secondary and unimportant.

In essence, you find a person who confirms your attachment style. This is why you should be cognizant of your own tendencies in this respect, as well as your potential partners. This way, you can make better decisions when finding a mate, and change your unhealthy attachment patterns if you do indeed have them. It is eminently possible to do this, to begin to have amazing and stable relationships with a little foresight and planning.

Understanding Committed Love and Relationships

All of this may sound like I'm downbeat on the relationship thing in general. Nothing could be further from the truth. There isn't anything more fulfilling and fruitful in this world than a healthy and balanced relationship. When committed love is harvested, it can last a lifetime. Two people in a genuine relationship may not always see fireworks when they kiss or hold hands. Instead, they may have occasional arguments, but they always do their best to resolve their problems and stay committed to one other. This is different to codependency.

A committed relationship is about sharing a life together. It involves loyalty, support, affection, kindness, and commitment. It is what Jungian writer Robert Johnson describes as "stirring the oatmeal" kind of love. It is when two people become willing to share their ordinary lives together and find meaning in simple, unromantic activities. These people do not feel the need to intensify the relationship by engaging in drama.

In other words, a committed relationship is more boring than exciting. It occurs when two people have grown to be companions. They are not addicted to each other, but they appreciate the others company more than anyone in the world. They have their own lives outside of the relationship. They pursue their own goals and engage in their own hobbies. They can function individually which makes their union that much stronger.

CHAPTER 4: JEALOUSY IN RELATIONSHIPS – HOW THIS CAN DRIVE YOUR PARTNER AWAY

"True love is a process of co-creation in which neither feels ownership or superiority. Jealousy is a highly destructive force for love and relationships"

(Jonathan Lockwood Huie)

In the previous chapters, we've explored the common traits of highly jealous people. If you notice yourself exhibiting these tendencies, its time to seriously assess your behavior and possibly change your ways. There is no shame in going to see a trained therapist if need be. Getting to the bottom and understanding the roots of your jealousy, as well as how you can overcome it and act more appropriately is paramount. If you do not change in this regard, it is highly likely that you will drive your partner away sooner or rather than later.

For example, if you are a frequently interrogate your partner, they will eventually grow tired of this questioning. Forcing them to tell you every detail of their work day, business trip, weekend out of town, or get-together with friends will ensure they feel constantly on trial. This will weaken your bond and destroy the trust in your relationship. Even if you are able to find some incriminating evidence and you feel vindicated, your relationship will still suffer due to this whole process.

As I have previously touched upon, another common trait of highly jealous people is to check the social media accounts of their partners. If you keep checking your partner's Facebook page, you will not just lose valuable time, you will also risk destroying your relationship in the process. Constantly obsessing each time you see a friend or even a stranger "like" and comment on your partner's status updates and photos. This only breads paranoia and leads to unfounded accusations towards your partner.

Likewise, if you follow your partner to the places they frequent, you will simply end up alienating them. People who follow their partners around only make themselves more jealous and insecure by doing so. They destroy their relationship as well as their own personal lives as they are no longer able to focus on their own work, studies, social life, family, etc.

Playing mind games can drive your partner away. Oftentimes, highly jealous people withdraw to see if their partners are still interested in them. They do this to "test" their partners and see how much they will react. However, its clear that this kind of behavior is unhealthy. It is not an effective way to send a message to your partner. If you want to convey a particular message, then you should just go ahead and say it instead of resorting to manipulative behaviors or tricks.

If you play mind games and withdraw from the relationship, it is likely that your partner will get the opposite message. Instead of doing or giving you what you want, they might think that you are no longer interested. They are also likely to begrudge you giving them a hard time, which can further worsen the situation as they withdraw from you. Rather than connect to each other, you practice reciprocal disconnection.

Furthermore, if you attempt to control your partner and take over every aspect of their life, you will simply end up ruining the relationship. If your jealousy causes you to demand that your partner cuts contact with friends, co-workers, clients, or even family members, they will almost certainly end up resenting you for this.

They may eventually realize that their life has degraded significantly due to obsessive jealousy. Demanding that your partner quit their job, stop engaging in past hobbies, move to a new city, cut contact with friends of the opposite gender, change the way they dress or talk and behave a certain way. Are all things which will ultimately push a partner away.

In fact, this is one of the biggest reasons why people leave altogether. If jealousy begins to affect the professional and social life of a partner, it is highly likely that they will go their own separate way. After all, people need to have careers, businesses, and a supportive social networks of their own. If these are taken away from them, they are likely to become resentful, miserable and isolated. Before long, they will feel suffocated in the relationship and prompt them to end it without delay.

This is obviously what we want to avoid. So having laid out the concepts and personality traits which lead to these undesirable consequences for a relationship, its now time to do something about it. The second part of this book deals with the strategies, mindsets and attitudes to properly deal with jealous behavior, and to overcome this destructive thought pattern once and for all!

PART 2: JEALOUSY - TECHNIQUES & PRACTICAL STRATEGIES TO COMBAT IT IN THE REAL WORLD

CHAPTER 5: RAISING YOUR OVERALL SELF-ESTEEM

"A competent and self-confident person is incapable of jealousy in anything. Jealousy is invariably a symptom of neurotic insecurity"

(Robert Heinlein)

The following passage is an adaptation from a chapter I wrote within *"Manipulation: A Psychologists Guide"*. However it is very apt for a discussion on jealousy, hence why I have included and expanded upon it here. I plan to write an entire book solely dedicated to the notion of raising overall self-confidence, especially with regards to women, as its such an important trait to develop.

If there is one true antidote to manipulative behavior in general, which includes jealousy, it is in raising ones own self-esteem and self-worth. Its the one overriding factor which protects you from pretty much all negative emotions which arise within you, as well as those emanating from others.

It's not some clever tactic or trick to deflect negative comments or anything like that, but rather raising your own self-confidence aids in diffusing the impact jealous actions have on you from the get-go. It inoculates you from ever being affected by negative behavior in the first place, as these forms of feelings are typically unconscious acts played out by those experiencing low confidence or temporary vulnerability.

Nobody will truly feel jealous if they have a high regard for themselves. In truth, nothing is more important than how you think and feel about yourself, that goes for relationships as well as life in general.

Handle Your Inner Critic

You have an inner critic, everyone does. Listening to this voice can aid in getting things done or helps you do the things that will gain acceptance from other people. But this inner critic can also kill your self-esteem if you let it. If you permit this egoic element of your personality to get out of hand.

I have described the importance of separating the "thinker" from the "feeler" within you in previous books. Needless to say that over thinking situations is not a good thing to be doing, I would go as far to say its the biggest plight on human civilization today.

It is normal for your inner voice to suggest both positive and negative thoughts. It's not about blocking out the noise. But rather analyzing what you are thinking, and if it is of any benefit to you? If it isn't, then it's important to prevent yourself from going down the rabbit hole of negative and spiraling imaginary scenarios.

Refocus those negative thoughts into something constructive and happier.

Cultivate a Gratitude Mindset

I used to think that being grateful for the sake of it was silly. Why would I appreciate everything I had in my life now? My goals were much larger and loftier. Wouldn't this be me thinking small and making do? Absolutely not! The mind works in a way to serve you more of what you are currently experiencing now. If you are constantly in a state of fear and worry, guess what. Your subconscious will simply serve you up more to be fearful and worried about.

On the other hand, if you are extremely positive and grateful in the here and now, the mind goes to work in finding you more of the same! The subconscious doesn't know the difference between feeling great because you just won the lottery, are being ecstatic simply to be alive. It works in feelings, emotions and imagery.

In this regard, learning to appreciate yourself, and all of the good things about your life, including your current relationship, is a great exercise to do. As a bonus to this, when you feel good about yourself and grateful for the things that you do have large or small, your mind won't have room to entertain negative thoughts.

Most of the suffering people go through in their lives is imaginary anyway. It's created from the dissonance between where they are and where they think they would like to be. But that is a false horizon, if you can't be happy with the journey then you will never be content with wherever you are heading, as there will always be the next thing when you get there.

Again, the trick is to be happy now. I know this sounds over simplified and easier said then done, but it really is the one thing which gave me the most joy in life when I was struggling with my business in the early days.

It has been shown that the top business professionals in the world do this (and all successful people in general). If they are currently at point 'B' in their lives, they do not look forward to point 'C' and say "look how far I have to go." As I mentioned previously, this is just a conceptual place like the horizon of the earth. Every time you try to chase after it, it disappears further into the distance.

Instead, what these people do is look back at point 'A' to where they started and say "hey, look how far I have come!" This is a subtle change of outlook but I promise you, if you do make this one adjustment in your thinking your whole outlook on life will change, and for the better. You will instantly start feeling grateful and satisfied with your current lot and much less frustrated with not yet being where you think you should be. Remember that the subconscious aims to serve you more of what you are felling right now. If you are abundantly happy and grateful for what is in your present existence, then it will go to work on finding other such situations to bring your way.

My previous business partner used to valet his car outside of his favorite restaurant in the city each week. However he could never understand why the parking attendant would always place his car two blocks away, instead of just across the road as he'd instructed. He would get so frustrated by having to wait an extra 5 minutes for his vehicle each time, it almost sent him into a frenzy. He would ask me what he should do about it, as he noticed I was much calmer in similar situations.

I simply asked him to think about it for a moment. What would he rather, be a well paid businessman who had the opportunity to valet his top of the range BMW at his favorite restaurant each week. But have to wait an extra five minutes for it each time he left. Or be the guy who has to valet cars and survive off tips for a living? His outlook on the situation immediately changed. "You're right he replied, what was I thinking? I'll give the guy a break from now on".

Put Things Into Writing

You can also write down the things that you like about yourself in a journal, the positive traits you have and situations they affect. When you are feeling low, or when the day is not turning out as well as you'd hoped, or when negative thoughts begin to creep into your mind, take out your list and re-read them. You can update this list daily, or whenever you discover something new and positive about yourself.

It's a good idea to start your day with going over these statements as they work a little like affirmations. You are cultivating the positive emotions surrounding these attributes or events and allowing you to feel them again in the here and now. Remember the brain has no way of telling the difference with regards to emotions I.e. the event could be happening now, 10 years ago or some way into the future!

Stop Being a Perfectionist

Aiming for perfection all of the time can be very destructive. Just like negative thoughts, perfectionism can paralyze you from getting things done due to your fear of not living up to a high standard you have set for yourself. This may also result in procrastination, thus, ending up not getting you the results you expected. This will bring your self-esteem crashing down if you let it.

Try making these alterations to your thinking to overcome perfectionism:

- *Strive for good enough.* **Stop aiming for perfection, remember nobody's perfect. When you aim for perfection all of the time, you won't finish any task because you'll either wait for the right time or continue to work on the task until it turns out flawless (which will never happen).**

- *Striving for perfection will only hurt you in the long run.* **Remind yourself that life is not a fairy tale that always ends with** *a happily ever after.* **Learn to manage your expectations, because after all, this is real life. You have managed to deal with everything life has thrown at you up until this point, how do I know this? Because you are still alive reading this today. The true curve balls in life you will never see coming so there is absolutely no point in worrying about them today. You will deal with them at the time as you always have done, so stop worrying.**

Look at Mistakes and Failure as Lessons

I will go into greater detail on this topic within the chapter on re-contextualization shortly. But for now, lets just say that it is inevitable that you will make mistakes from time to time. You will fail on some days. But the good thing about experiencing failures and committing mistakes is that there are lessons to be gleaned from them all.

There will always be positives you can take from every situation, you just have to find out what they are. Learn from them and internalize these things and come back stronger. "You either win or you learn" as they say. I couldn't agree more.

Similar to this, you always need to be trying something new. Get out of your comfort zone as much and as often as possible. This is the only true route to feeling content and successful in life. In having new experiences and learning new things that will feed into your positive confidence and self-esteem feedback loops.

They do not need to be big and scary all of the time, just small wins, incremental progress will do the job. As long as you are moving in the right direction, that is all that counts.

Stop Comparing Yourself to Others

You will never be good enough if you keep on comparing yourself with other people. You will never win because there's always someone better or there is always something more valuable to attain out there. You are only ever in a competition with yourself, to improve on the version of you from yesterday or a year ago.

Remember to always look back at 'A', not forward to 'C'. Look at how far you have come as a person with regards to your development. Other people are on their own journey, let them get on with it. Only you walk in your shoes, be proud of that and keep treading your own path.

Be Around People who are Supportive of You

This is fairly obvious but most people still do not take as much notice of this concept as they should. It's simple, don't hang around negative people who only see the things that you have done wrong. This includes jealous people!

It's said that you are the aggregate of the five people you most commonly associate with. Or show me your friends and I'll show you your future type of deal. This is because we adjust our behavior in line with these people accordingly. That goes for everything from mannerisms, speaking styles to the amount of money everyone is making. You will adjust your thermostat in all categories to usually meet the mean of this peer group.

So try to be around positive and high performance people, those who are willing to support you and lift you up. This is easier said then done with regards to close friends and family, but you do have to draw the line somewhere. Be with people who will pick you up when you fall and help you get back on your feet again.

Make a conscious effort to only socialize with those who encourage your progress and feed your confidence. It goes without saying that the jealous types will have a hard time with this. So be ruthless, remove them from your social groups or at least cut down your exposure to them whenever possible. Rising above needless gossip goes a long way in preventing the green eyed monster from ever rearing its ugly head!

CHAPTER 6: HOW TO DEFUSE JEALOUSY TRIGGERS WHEN THEY ARISE WITHIN YOU

"Nobody can hurt me without my permission"

(Mahatma Gandhi)

Raising your overall self-esteem is a great way to overcome almost all negative thinking. It allows you to rise above the pettiness and low level emotions in such a way that these feelings hardly register when they do arise. However, nobody is 100% confident all of the time. Everybody experiences peaks and troughs when developing positive thinking patterns. I have worked on myself tirelessly over the years, but still suffer these momentary lapses in confidence from time to time. That's just part and parcel of being human.

Fortunately there are a few tools we can call upon in such instances. One of which involves identifying and defusing jealousy triggers when they show up. To snuff them out before they develop into full scale negative thinking spirals. This method isn't exclusive to combating jealousy, but all destructive thought patterns. However, the following are some of the ways we can use this technique to appropriately deal with the feelings of envy when they do arise:

1. Be open and honest about your thoughts and feelings.

If you are feeling uncertain or insecure in your relationship, you have to have an honest conversation with your partner. Refrain from playing mind games or expecting your partner to read yours. If you want to convey a message, you have to be direct and to the point.

It is all right to talk about your desires, concerns, and doubts. However, you should talk in a way that will not make your partner feel accused. Refrain from making gestures which can provoke your partner to feel attacked, such as finger pointing and the like. You can ease any tension by being open and understanding, as well as allowing your partner to explain his/her side.

2. Do not act on your feelings right away

Feelings tend to come and go throughout the day. Hence, you should not act upon your feelings immediately, especially at the extremes. Whenever you begin to feel a strong emotion, either good or bad, pause for a second and take a few deep breaths. Carefully evaluate what you are experiencing and find out why it has arisen within you. Think of the possible consequences of acting on this particular feeling. Chances are, you will later regret what you said or did if you chose to act without this momentary contemplation.

Hence, the next time you feel jealous, simply assess the situation first. Do not do or say whatever comes to your mind in the first instance. Evaluate your thoughts carefully as we generally change the way we view these instances after just a few seconds to ponder them. Be open to feasible reasons and explanations. For example, if you see your spouse talking to his ex-wife, you may feel jealous and tempted to confront them both. Don't jump to conclusions, there is almost always a benign explanation for such occurrences.

3. Appreciate your own self.

Before you met your partner, you were your own person. You were likely happy and content with life. You did whatever you pleased for the most part. You had everything you needed. Whenever you feel jealous of someone else, such as a friend or co-worker of your partner, you have to remind yourself that your partner is not your whole life. You have family, friends, and a career. You have your own goals and interests. You are perfectly whole. Your partner is just a very nice addition to your life. By realizing this, you can once again rebuild your self-esteem.

You have to know that you are a wonderful person. You possess great qualities which attracted your partner in the first place. Never forget that.

4. Allow your wounds to heal.

Many people experience extreme levels of jealousy due to negative past experiences. They may have experienced abusive and dysfunctional relationships in which they were cheated on, abandoned, used, or psychologically abused. They may have been hurt so badly that they find it difficult to let go and trust another person again.

So, the next time you find yourself making unreasonable assumptions about your partner's whereabouts or activities, pause for a while and evaluate why you are feeling this way. Did your previous partner come home late each night because he was seeing another woman? If so, you should remember that you are no longer with that person. You have a new partner who might simply be doing overtime at work or is stuck in traffic. Again, the benefit of the doubt must be given for your own sanity.

You have to move forward and let go of your past hurts, guilt, anger, and other such feelings. You need to understand the reasons, roots, and triggers for your jealousy in order to grow and be healthy. Whenever you start to feel jealous, you have to make a conscious decision to heal old wounds. You have to remind yourself that your past and present are not the same and that you can make your present relationship work.

5. Trust your partner and yourself.

When you enter a relationship, you have to accept that there are risks involved. No relationship is perfect. No person is perfect. There is also no way to see the future and find out exactly how things will play out. If you want to be happy, you need to be optimistic about your relationship. Refrain from thinking and expecting the worst. Act with faith instead of fear.

Remember that what is true for you, is ultimately true. So, if you believe that your relationship will eventually end, you will unconsciously do the things to sabotage it. You have already imprinted this outcome in your mind. It will just then become a self-fulfilling prophecy.

You have to trust in your partner and in yourself that both of you can make the relationship work. Accept the fact that you cannot control your partner. Remember that no matter how hard you try to keep him/her away from temptations, he/she is still their own person and needs the freedom to express themselves too.

You have to trust in yourself that you will be all right no matter what happens in your relationship. Even if your partner is unfaithful or leaves you, you are still a wonderful person who is worthy of being loved. You can still find a new partner and be happy in a new relationship. By giving yourself this reassurance, your feelings of jealousy can take a backseat and your self-esteem receives a boost once more.

6. Tame your imagination.

I have touched on this in previous chapters already. But if you have a wild imagination, you really have to find a way to keep it in check. A reckless imagination can ensure that jealousy germinates and grows. Hence, you should recognize the times when you are engaging in negative self-talk and blowing things out of proportion. Refrain from playing events over and over in your head. Obsessing over perceived wrongful events does no good whatsoever.

Aim to tame wild mind chatter by practicing mindfulness meditation. You have to train yourself to focus on the present moment and simply acknowledge your jealous thoughts. Instead of holding on to them, let go. Mindfulness meditation can help clear your head and allow you to have more rational thoughts.

7. Take a reality check.

Similar to the above, identify your jealousy triggers and evaluate them carefully. Are they truly realistic or are they simply by-products of your imagination? Assess your obsessive thoughts. Replace conspiracy theories with real facts. Be objective rather than subjective. Oftentimes, people get carried away with their jealousy, so they are no longer able to think clearly and rationally.

One such way to force a reality check is to write things down. When you write out your thoughts, you can evaluate them better. Its a cathartic and calming experience. Each time you begin to feel jealous, write down everything that comes to mind. What are the things or actions that you plan to do? Why do you feel jealous? What is the triggering factor causing you to feel this way? What is your observed reality of the situation?

For example, you and your partner made plans to go out of town this weekend. Suddenly, he cancels on you. Then tells you that he has to go on a business trip and meet with a client instead. This makes you upset and jealous. You begin to contemplate all of the ways your partner could be acting to justify these feelings.

Again, its simply about assessing things rationally. Don't let yourself feel the emotions of jealousy until your other half gives you a real reason for doing so. Don't hasten the demise of your current relationship for momentary insecurity. Remember to trust and communicate with your partner clearly. This will defuse 99% of problems when they do arise. Communication really is king, which leads us very nicely on to the next chapter.

CHAPTER 7: LEARNING TO TRUST & RECONNECT – COMMUNICATION ADVICE TO REPAIR RELATIONSHIPS

"He that is jealous is not in love"

(Saint Augustine)

A well functioning romantic relationship is one of, if not the most rewarding thing in the world. It's literally heaven on earth if you can get it right, which is why its so worthwhile striving to achieve. However, we live in the real world where sadly these unions can break down much more frequently then we'd like.

When this is the case, we need to do the adequate work to repair the damage. If you are in a relationship, in essence, you need to do your share. Maintaining a relationship is not easy, it requires much give and take. There has to be open lines of communication, honesty, loyalty, and commitment to give yourself a fighting chance.

According to statistics, 60% of second marriages and 41% of first marriages end up in divorce. According to author

Dr. Sue Johnson, expectation mismatch and stress of living causes couples to have problems for the most part. Their previous attachment issues also bring problems into their current relationships far to frequently.

No relationship is perfect — but if you are willing to work on it, it is possible to make a union last for a lifetime. My parents are a shining example of this. High school sweethearts who are about to celebrate 55 years of marriage. Granted we live in different times today, however its still possible to cultivate such a relationship with the right ingredients. This often requires a large degree of trust and communication skills. If you find yourself struggling with this, the following is some advice to help you reconnect and repair your relationship once more:

1. *Hear your partner out and stay present.*

Allow your partner to speak. Do not take over the conversation. When your partner begins to express themselves, listen intently to what they are saying, as opposed to simply waiting for your turn to talk. Stay present and refrain from thinking of other things or finding ways to undermine your partner. Bring down your defenses and be open to reconciliation. Keep in mind that it is not about defending yourself, but rather attempting to understand your partner in the most sincere way possible.

Do not allow your pride or ego to dictate your decisions. Since your goal is to repair your relationship, you have to be willing to forgive. You do not necessarily have to forget what has transpired. However, you should be willing to move forward and refrain from continually bringing up past mistakes. Let your partner know that you hear and accept their unmet needs and that you are willing to make the necessary changes.

2. Empathize with your partner.

Along similar lines, you should not just listen to your partner. You have to put yourself in their shoes in order to fully understand what they are trying to say. When you empathize with your partner, you can fulfill their needs much better.

You have to understand their feelings as well as pay attention to your own. When your partner opens up to you, you should listen but think twice before giving advice. Sometimes, people just want someone to listen to them. They are not seeking to have their problems solved. So, unless your partner asks for it, you should refrain from giving advice or proposing a solution too soon.

In addition, you have to watch your tone and choice of words. If you are not careful, your partner may view your advice as judgmental or overly critical. This will only make things worse. You have to stay emotionally engaged as well as express compassion to provide connection and comfort.

3. Address concerns and be willing to make changes.

You have to be willing to address the needs of your partner as well as make the necessary changes in your own actions, not simply paying lip service to what is being said. For example, if your partner feels anxious, you may make an effort to call more often to let them know that you are thinking of them. You may also want to do things which make them feel more appreciated. Its the little things which make the biggest impact here.

Your partner will feel respected and valued if they see you taking their concerns seriously. This will result in a positive cycle in your relationship. Your partner will be more willing to do their part in mending the union as a result. So make the first gesture on this, I promise it will make a big difference.

4. Love as unconditionally as you can.

If you love someone, your feelings for that person aren't jeopardized by momentary and menial negative thought patterns. If you are experiencing problems in the relationship, you can reconnect with your partner by recalling their good qualities and the good times you had together. Remember the things which attracted you in the first place. These should be plentiful, but you only need one reminder to rekindle the spark you once felt.

Forgive your partner and yourself for the things you did to damage your relationship. Do not hesitate to reach out or show positive gestures. Show your love and concern. When you love unconditionally, your expressions are not contingent on outside forces. Instead, they involve support, forgiveness, caring, and understanding. If you still have unresolved trust issues, you should think of the ways to rebuild your trust.

Then again, remember that loving unconditionally is not the same as being a doormat. You should not allow anyone, including your partner, to disrespect you and walk all over you. If you love yourself and your partner, you will draw healthy boundaries. But once again, the whole is greater than the sum of the parts when this works!

5. Make improving your communication priority number one

Communication is probably the most vital skill anybody can learn in life in general, and no more so when it comes to romantic relationships. A lack of communication almost always causes problems between couples, and often terminally too. When you communicate with your partner, you have to gain perspective on what matters to them. You should not just be mindful of your own interests. You need to also practice thoughtful transparency, which is crucial for trust building. You have to create an environment in which your partner can feel safe and secure.

Do not forget to contribute gratitude. Specific, personal, and sincere appreciation elevates communication and builds trust once more. You can give your partner gifts or tokens of appreciation on a regular basis to make them feel loved. You do not have to wait for your anniversary or holidays for these shows of affection. Simply reminding your partner that you love them and that you are thankful for them being in your life, goes a long way.

Furthermore, you should align your words with your actions. If you say something, you have to act in accordance to it. In other words, you have to "walk your talk" to build trust. Do not say something and then do the opposite. Your behavioral integrity can have a significant impact on your relationship and the way your partner sees you. So make this open and honest communication a priority, and everything else will fall into place that much easier.

CHAPTER 8: EMOTIONAL RE-CONTEXTUALIZATION - GAINING PERSPECTIVE

"Love looks through a telescope, envy, through a microscope"

(Josh Billings)

Everybody has heard the popular NLP phrase "The map in not the territory" regarding the true nature of reality. It suggests that things are not set in stone within our physical existence. But rather it is perception, or more accurately, projection which determines our materialistic world. Quantum mechanics has been demonstrating this for almost a century now.

Observations such as the double slit experiment illustrate that atoms (which make up all material things) are not solid structures at their base levels. They are vibrating particles which exist in quantum "superpositions" whose wave functions do not collapse until a conscious being observes them. Crazy stuff right.

But what does this have to do with the relationships we have and how we feel about ourselves in general? The answer is, everything. The way you view your current situation and outlook on life dictates the way in which it will play out. Its a mindset switch that can make all the difference to our happiness and well-being.

Let me give you an idea of what I mean here. If I were to make the statement that "A man is jumping". What is the first image which comes to mind? You likely envisaged some chap jumping up and down in the street or maybe in some sporting context like playing tennis. What if I then inserted "A man is jumping on a diving board". Now your image has changed. Another layer of information has been added to the picture.

What about "A man is jumping on a dead dog or jumping in front of a train to save a small child". Once again the image is altered radically. How about "A man is jumping to conclusions or down his wife's throat". This one might seem familiar! The point is, we can re-contextualize these statements ad infinitum.

So how can we utilize this concept to serve us better in our relationships? I eluded to this previously, but one of the most important areas to do this, is with the set-backs and obstacles we face. We have contextualized problems as bad or negative, when in fact we should be doing the opposite. If we are indeed in a healthy and well functioning relationship, these issues point to genuine areas where we can improve on things.

Positive outcomes are literally lying on the other side of unsolved problems. Henry Ford once stated that "Thinking is the hardest work there is, that's why so few people do it". I couldn't agree more. We are all guilty of becoming lazy in our thinking which can lead us to becoming complacent in fixing the issues we need to face. This is evidently clear when it comes to ironing out minor differences between you and your significant offer, before they grow into something more sinister.

To do this, it simply requires a small re-contextualization in your mind. It just takes a thought pattern interrupt when these issues show up. They should be a light bulb which switches on in your head signifying that you have found another gateway to progress. These should be exciting moments as you know that growth is just around the corner for you and your partner. Enjoy these moments, embrace them, and you'll find that you will be moving to new levels in your relationship in no time.

In addition to this, its also beneficial to re-contextualize your relationship in general. I have mentioned many of these concepts already. But you have to stop viewing the partnership in a codependent manner. Do not overvalue your significant other to the point you become unhealthily vulnerable. Likewise, do not degrade yourself in anyway and maintain an independent element to your life as well.

It all boils down to having a mindful relationship. One which is constantly improving as the weeks and months go by. But won't be debilitating to either party if it were to end. Retain your individuality at all costs and a proximity which keeps things both intimate and exclusive, yet with enough space to keep the attraction going. Again, this simply requires a small re-contextualization in your mind. But one well worth making.

CONCLUSION

"Envy is the art of counting the other fellows blessings instead of your own"

(Harold Coffin)

I began this book by pointing out the traits of highly jealous individuals. Whether you view yourself in this camp or not is unimportant. We are all human, we are emotional creatures by very nature and everyone will experience episodes of jealousy and envy at some stage in life. It's not about suppressing these feelings, but rather changing the way we react to these instances when they do arise. Its about exploring that space between stimulus and response. Identifying why you are feeling the way you are and rationally appraising the situation in a pragmatic fashion.

I know this sounds somewhat cold hearted and easier said then done. Especially if you have recently been hurt in a romantic setting. But it really is the only way to set yourself free from the pain of these negative thinking spirals which are so easy to fall into. Much of this comes naturally with age, wisdom and experience. Whilst much can also be negated by raising ones overall self-esteem and self-worth.

Its difficult not to repeat all of the cliched self-help style sound bites and metaphors when discussing the topic of envy and jealousy. Although many ring true. "Remember that people only rain on your parade because they are jealous of your sun and tired of their shade". This is simply another way of stating that perception is projection. People rarely react to others in their environment due to what they are seeing, they react with regards to what they are experiencing inside of themselves. This is largely an unconscious act, which is why you can't become angry at folks when they do this.

In fact, there is literally no point in spending a single second analyzing why people are acting negatively towards you or others for no apparent reason. They are simply working through their own baggage, so don't stand in their way. Where I do believe it is worth assessing jealous behavior though, is within intimate relationships, as it seems to be so prevalent here. That is why I have focused on this heavily within the second section of this book. If you have been following along with the tips laid out within those chapters, you should have a good idea of how to combat this. It really isn't a hard task or something which requires much effort at all when done correctly.

If you are building legitimate trust between yourself and your partner, developing great communication skills, as well as giving the other person enough breathing space to live, then you'll be just fine. This will breed a confidence in not only yourself, but mutually within the partnership also. Suddenly instances which may have triggered a jealous response within you, now elicit no such feelings whatsoever. You rise above them and simply move on with your day.

As I always state, work on yourself and you will find that almost all of your troubles will no longer register as such. If you are attempting to get out of debt, don't focus on the debt itself. What you focus on creates more of it within your physical reality. Instead, you should concentrate on creating revenue streams to make more money. Then at some point the debt will be paid off by default. Its exactly the same concept with regards to personal and emotional growth. Do not focus of the negative points of your personality. Dial in on the positives and cultivate them to the point that the negatives simply disappear without an ounce of effort on your part.

I'm not suggesting to ignore legitimate warning signs that your partner may be unfaithful or abusive for instance. But give them the benefit of the doubt at all costs until you do find something concrete. Always remember, that you are not doing this for them. You are doing it for your own sanity and peace of mind.

Finally, remember that we are all flawed in someway. We are all struggling with some form of mental anguish. It just comes down to the severity of your case and your ability to deal with it. Jealousy is really only an extension of social anxiety and can be alleviated in much the same way I.e. by adopting a more rational view on things as well as raising your overall self-worth.

Hopefully you now have a better idea of how to deal with this yourself. So make sure you are doing a little each day to stay on the path to achieving a positive, jealousy free mindset. Do it for your own sake, in addition to improving the quality of your current and future relationships. They can be amazing if you wish them to be. Just remember to enjoy the journey, and I wish you the very best of luck along the way.

BONUS CHAPTER

(From 'Emotional Intelligence: A Psychologist's Guide')

CHAPTER 4: TAKING INVENTORY OF YOUR EMOTIONAL STATE

"Educating the mind without educating the heart is no education at all"

(Aristotle)

One of the most important things you can do when initially starting out on your emotional intelligence enhancing journey is to take stock of what you are currently feeling. There is no right or wrong answers here in terms of what come up. As our limbic legacy show us, humans are inherently emotional creatures and suppressing them is almost impossible to do entirely.

However you do have control over the way you react to these tendencies, the thoughts and behaviors after the fact. The following factors should help you take a closer look into how to identify and deal with these feelings when they do arise to ultimately move you to the next level in your E.Q. journey.

Acknowledge Your Emotions

The first thing to do when attempting to increase your personal E.Q. levels is to get good at acknowledging and perceiving the emotions that you are feeling. This is the starting point for every model and framework of E.Q.

Whenever I feel an emotion arise within me I always take a pause and acknowledge its presence, I take a moment and really feel it so I can understand and label it in my mind. This isn't the same as reacting or acting upon the emotion just yet, but I want to know why it may have arisen and if it could be useful to me. If it's a feeling of anger, fear or frustration I do not deny or try to hide it, but instead acknowledge its presence and dismiss it as not being productive and move on.

If you start to dwell on emotions such as these you will quickly fall into a negative spiral thought process that will have you framing everything in a pessimistic light before you know it. I used to play out entire imaginary scenarios in my head of something going badly and the knock-on effects that I 'knew' it would have, only to realize that it NEVER worked out that badly and that I'd fabricated it all in my mind. Sound familiar?

If on the other hand it is an emotion of excitement, joy or anticipation, I also pause for a moment, acknowledge and label what it is that I'm feeling and try to cultivate and utilize it if I think it will benefit the situation such as situational empathy (which we will get onto later).

It is also important to take responsibility for these emotions that you are feeling either way, good or bad. Know that it is something inside of you which is eliciting such a response and that you have to deal with it and not sweep it under the carpet so to speak. This is usually the most challenging step for people, but it is also the most rewarding. Yes it maybe some outside influence or stimulus that sparked the response in the first place, but remember that the emotions you are feeling are coming from within you and that it's your responsibility to deal with them

Understand That You Are Not Your Emotions

So following on from that, you also need to constantly remind yourself that the emotions which arise within you and the conscious entity which interprets them are two very different things. Most people walk around in somewhat of a waking sleep for the most part completely at the mercy of any feeling, thought or emotion that pops into their head.

You have to understand that many thoughts and emotions will pass through you almost on a second by second basis, but again it's entirely your choice on how you perceive and choose to react to them.

There is also a very large egoic element to this process as well. Thoughts and feelings of jealously for another person or fear of performing a task is really just your ego trying to keep your preconceived notions about the world intact and keep you operating within your comfort zone. This is a topic for much greater discussion i.e. regarding the tactics to counteract such self-sabotaging behavior, but needless to say that detaching yourself from your overall emotional state is very a beneficial thing to do.

Learn to Forgive Yourself & Others

"Life becomes easier when you learn to accept an apology you never got"

(Robert Brault)

Again, along the same lines as letting go of a negative emotion that arises within you, people have a great tendency to hold onto what they perceive to be negative acts that they have either committed themselves or others against them. Holding onto this ill feeling again serves absolutely no purpose to you in the immediate future and certainly not the long run. *Holding onto anger is like drinking poison and expecting the other person to die*" as the Buddha so aptly put it.

If there was one thing that got me ahead in my business life so quickly it was this concept. Once I stopped getting caught up with what I thought I deserved from a situation or others around me and started pushing ahead regardless, I made so much more progress. You can't stop and throw stones at every dog that barks, and that includes yourself when you mess up.

This isn't just applicable to adult and business life either, it's relates to everyone young or old. If I had taken heed of this advice when I was growing up I know I would have had better overall relationships with school/college friends and family alike. That's not to say things were necessarily that bad, but they could have been better, or at least I could have saved myself a great deal of heart ache and stress along the way.

Don't Get Involved in Negative Self-Talk

As I mentioned above, letting negative self talk get out of hand is a very bad habit to take up. I would say that it is the one thing that plagues humanity more than anything. We often talk ourselves out of things before we've had a chance to start them. Again this comes down to letting negative thoughts and emotions cloud our thinking to a point of almost no escape. You have to stop this in its tracks as quickly as possible if you want to build high overall levels of emotional intelligence.

This also includes negative self-talk and 'gossip' regarding other people. In danger of sounding like one of your parents or school teachers here, you don't need me to tell you this is a worthless exercise and one that will ultimately bring your E.Q. level down with it. No one is perfect; just make a point of catching yourself when you start to talk in this way.

Also along the same lines as the above, you must try and do your best not to judge others where ever possible. This actually freed me greatly in a psychological sense when I managed to stop doing it a few years ago. I never thought of myself as an overly judgmental person but I still realized I would do it from time to time. But stopping myself altogether from judging anyone I came across in even the smallest way saves me so much mental energy and almost certain daily miss judgment.

Nowadays I simply let others go about their day in their own way without even the slightest judging thought about their behavior. That is not to say that I tolerate bad behavior or that I do not try and empathize with people and attempt to understand their situation better, which is critical to building fruitful relationships. But I don't judge them with regards to how they got to where they are, I never walked in their shoes or went through the struggles they did so I let them do the talking on this one.

Again this isn't some "holier than thou" situation, I'm not perfect and do very occasionally catch myself automatically judging someone. I just now catch it very early and stop myself in my tracks straight away. It's so much more liberating when you do.

BONUS CHAPTER

(From 'NLP: A Psychologist's Guide')

CHAPTER 7: LOOP BREAKS & PATTERN INTERRUPTS

The brain is undoubtedly an extremely complex organ within the human body. It is required to perform an incredible number of calculations every second even during mundane tasks like guiding the various parts of the body for movement in simple motor skills all the way to making crucial and complex decisions in real time. The brain undertakes millions of these interconnected decisions every single day thereby making it one of the most powerful pieces of biological machinery we have.

However we still do not fully understand the extent of it's complexity and inner workings. One thing we do know is that the brain is solely responsible for enabling people to develop thought patterns and habits that ultimately dictate not only their daily behaviors but also their thinking patterns. It does this in an attempt to optimize a person's day-to-day movements and thought processes, but these short cuts aren't always beneficial.

In order to form these "loops" or "patterns" the brain undertakes several processes that help it both develop a certain habit and make it a part of routine life. In this segment, we will start by taking a brief look at the meaning of cognition in general, which is fairly critical when it comes to NLP. Cognition is simply the study of how the brain perceives information and represents it within the persons mind. It tells us how the brain functions and helps in putting that information to use.

The branch of study that deals with establishing a relationship between learning and cognition is known as neuropsychology, an area of study I once specialized in myself. Neurology has intrigued scientists for as long as the concept has been around with many psychologists having studied its intricacies for decades now. Right from classical conditioning described by Pavlov and John Watson to the operant conditioning of B F Skinner, each one presented theories that described how the human brain works and learns.

It is no secret that a person's daily habits and thinking routines will ultimately dictate how productive and successful they are. However habits are impartial, they will either help a person attain their desired results and remain persistent in pursuing them. Or they will ensure they continue getting the average/poor results they have always gotten. As Dr Bandler pointed out "Brains aren't designed to get results; they just go in directions".

In terms of general behavior it is usually just a case of learning your ABC's so to speak i.e. learning the sequence of the Antecedent, Behavior and Consequence. This concept was originally based on Skinner's model of cognition, antecedent, behavior and consequence being the three main steps involved in developing a habit. In a nutshell they are described as follows:

Antecedents

Antecedents are stimuli that precede a behavior or reaction. They are situations and circumstances that cause a person to behave in a certain manner. Antecedents determine the outcome of a certain behavior by inducing it automatically.

In simpler terms, antecedents are people and situations that solicit a certain reaction or behavior. They are what lay down the basis for habits, they hold the key to how a person reacts to any given situation.

Antecedents are studied to know whether the reaction is a result of positive reinforcement or punishment by and large. Having this knowledge makes it easier to predict future behavior. It is fairly simple to manipulate antecedents in order to evoke the desired behavior.

Behavior

The second component within the habit development model is behavior. Behavior is the response provided to the stimulus. It is meant to serve two main purposes namely to get something that a person desires or to avoid getting something they do not. It is important to note that almost all behavior is learned from significant others. Some is reactionary but all is observable and measurable.

This means that behavior is both visible to others and is a reflection of the person's mind. For example, if a person is angry then their behavior will come through in the form of a changed facial expression or an angry physical reaction. This behavior differs from person to person and is not constant, but rather based on their learned behavior through observing others during past experiences.

As I mention, behavior is also measurable. This means that it is possible for another person to describe the behavior after observation. For example, a person can observe another person getting angry and describe his reaction. This behavior can be altered to give away a desirable outcome.

Consequence

Consequence is the final component and is a result of the behavior phase. It can be viewed as the environment's reaction to a certain behavior. A consequence will be a direct result of the behavioral action. For example, if a person reacts to a certain situation in a negative manner then the consequence is bound to be negative. Say a person slams a vase on the floor out of anger then it is obvious that the vase will break and the person will have to clean it up. Consequence is also measurable just like behavior.

Basically if you are fully aware of the process I described above you can alter it for your own benefit. It involves understanding the cues, following a routine and availing the consequence/reward. The key here is to aim for the desired results but change the antecedent and rewards, then the behavior will automatically change accordingly.

For example, if you are trying to learn a new skill, but buying books in order to achieve this is not inspiring you enough to study the material then changing over to online classes may inspire you to better effect.

Similarly, you can also change the reward in order to modify the behavior. For example, when trying to excel in a competitive exam, you can look forward to treating yourself to a toy/clothes you have wanted to buy for a long time. Both can work as a motivating factor for you to modify the behavior enough.

The above method works great for changing more general behavioral patterns I find. However we are more concerned with the thinking habits here as opposed to just the behavioral, although they somewhat go hand in hand. That is what real NLP seeks to accomplish. For that you need to view things in a slightly different way, to adopt another approach.

TOTE Process

With regards to the thinking process in NLP there is a similar structure that the mind follows. It's sometimes described as the path of least resistance approach and is made up of four components the Trigger, Operation, Test and Exit. I'll elaborate on each in a little more detail below:

Trigger

Similar to the ABC sequence of behavior learning I described above, the TOTE process starts with an antecedent or cue known here as the trigger. In NLP it's also called the 'Anchor' from time to time and once again relates to the impetus or stimulus which starts off the pattern.

Operation

The operation once again like the ABC process, relates to the behavior portion of the pattern and the thinking habit that we undertake.

Test

However this time the mind performs a 'test' of that preceding behavior to identify whether the intended outcome was met or not. Did the person get the desired result from that action? If the answer is 'no', then the person will continue through with the behavior cycle until they do.

Exit

If the answer was 'yes' to the test stage, then a person will simply move on with their behavior and proceed to close this thinking pattern loop so to speak. This completion stage must happen in order to not continually go round in circles.

This is how we typically form habits in thinking which can be very powerful cycles especially if built and reinforced over a long period of time. It isn't necessarily a bad thing if this thinking loop is genuinely a beneficial one, but if it is not then it can be quite destructive. We can see this quite clearly in individuals with high obsessive compulsive tendencies (OCD).

In any case these cycles can be reasonably difficult to break but it's imperative that you do so in order to move on from a negative cycle. That is one of the main tenants of NLP, breaking these negative thought patterns to replace with better and more beneficial ones. This process certainly played a critical role to my overall success. When I really learnt how to pattern interrupt.

Thought Pattern Interrupts

The idea here is to disrupt a negative thought pattern as early on in the cycle/sequence as possible, more specifically between the trigger and the operation. Regardless it must be completed before the testing phase of the condition, to say that you must disrupt it before the mind tries to test the original operation pattern otherwise any attempt to break the sequence will be of little use as the pattern is almost completed.

The pattern interrupts aren't that difficult to implement and it is simply about stopping your train of thought and thinking about something different, butting in on your own thought process/conversation you are having within your own head.

Like Richard Bandler suggests, we are simply trying to change the direction of the mind and reprogram it as we do. You are not removing the old pattern per se, but rather redirecting around it.

Go big!

The idea is to make this interrupt as big and bold as possible. If there is one mistake I see from people who try this method is that they are too weak with their disrupting action and it isn't enough to fully divert their thinking. Especially if it is a long term entrenched habit of thought they are trying to break.

Try a loud clap of the hands or loud cough. If the cycle which is trying to be broken is a negative thought process with depressive emotions attached to it, then try breaking the pattern with a little dance/jig or a laugh. Try to inject humor into the disrupt as it is completely counter to the original and unwanted behavior and congruent with the newer, happier thought process.

Timing is Everything

As I described above, timing is everything here. You need to ensure you catch the trigger phase as accurately as you can as it will be key to identifying when you need to employ the pattern disrupt. In essence this should be directly after and as soon as possible following on from when the trigger is spotted.

However in reality this is likely to be a very short period of time so you really have to be a keen observant throughout the day to catch them when they do occur. For me it was usually some thought or memory which popped into my head that would start the cycle, especially the negative ones.

If I let it continue, my emotions and physiology would start to change when in it would be too late. I have now learnt to catch this right before this transition takes place i.e right after the trigger thought/memory and replace my momentary operation/behavior to a more positive one.

Rinse & Repeat

However that is simply not enough in my experience, just catching the cycle once. The real payoff comes from repeating this cycle over and over until the new behavior pattern becomes habitual and you start to see the results you are looking for.

So make sure you perform whatever interrupt you have chosen until it becomes second nature to you, until you no longer have to think about it. You have to bring the skill into the "Unconscious Competence" phase when performing it. That is when the new direction of thought and subsequent behavior will really take hold.

This general approach was taken from hypnotherapists such as Milton Erickson who used pattern interrupts to disrupt the waking thinking patterns of their participants. They would lead a persons inner monologue down a familiar path before disrupting the line of questioning leaving the persons unconscious mind waiting for the logical next step of the pattern to occur, but it never comes. This can be a powerful enough confusion of the mind which puts a certain percentage of the population into a hypnotic trance.

You are not attempting to go that far with yourself and it's almost impossible to do it on your own, but the general thought pattern interrupt is designed to work along the same lines. But this time to disrupt a familiar negative thought pattern such as anger and replace with a more positive and beneficial one.